10-minute
SEASONAL
CRAFTS
for
SPRING

ANNALEES LIM

WINDMILL
BOOKS
New York

Published in 2015 by Windmill Books, An Imprint of Rosen Publishing
29 East 21st Street, New York, NY 10010

Senior Editor for Wayland: Julia Adams
US Editor: Joshua Shadowens
Craft stylist: Annalees Lim
Designer: Emma Randall
Photographer: Simon Pask, N1 Studios

Photo Credits: All step-by-step craft photography: Simon Pask, N1 Studios; images used
throughout for creative graphics: Shutterstock.

Library of Congress Cataloging-in-Publication Data

Lim, Annalees, author.
 10-minute seasonal crafts for spring / by Annalees Lim.
     pages cm. — (10-minute seasonal crafts)
 Includes index.
 ISBN 978-1-4777-9206-3 (library binding) — ISBN 978-1-4777-9207-0 (pbk.) —
ISBN 978-1-4777-9208-7 (6-pack)
1. Handicraft—Juvenile literature. 2. Spring—Juvenile literature. I. Title.
TT160.L48493 2015
745.5—dc23

                              2013048367

Manufactured in the United States of America

CPSIA Compliance Information: Batch #WS14WM: For Further Information contact Windmill Books, New York, New York at 1-866-478-0556

Contents

Spring

Spring is one of the seasons of the year. The months of spring are March, April and May. During spring, the days start getting longer and the weather gets warmer and often more sunny.

Spring is the time of year when things start to grow. Seeds germinate, and can grow into plants or small trees, called saplings. You can see the bare trees of winter turning green with lots of new leaves, too. Spring is also the time when many animals are born or hatch from eggs.

You can see lots of different weather in spring. It can be rainy, sunny or windy. Don't let that stop you from going outside to explore. Rubber boots are perfect for splashing about in spring showers. And don't forget to bring a waterproof jacket!

In this book you will find out about lots of natural materials you can collect while you're outside, and how to make great crafts out of them. But remember to be careful about what you collect. A lot is still growing and should not be picked. Anything that you do collect should be washed before you use it.

Fluffy Sheep

If you get a chance to visit a farm or take a walk across some fields you might spot some newly born sheep. They are called lambs. Make your own countryside scene when you are at home by using some grass and cotton balls.

You will need:

- A piece of blue card stock
- Glue and a paintbrush
- cotton balls
- Black card stock
- Brightly colored paper
- Grass
- Scissors
- Pencil

Paint some hill shapes onto a blue piece of card stock using some glue.

Sprinkle the grass over the glue and shake off the excess.

Lots of baby animals are born in spring. Try using the grass to make a nest and the cotton balls to make some chirping birds that have just hatched from their eggs.

3 Stick three cotton balls onto the grassy hills using glue.

4 Make the heads and feet by cutting out the shapes from black card stock. Stick them to the cotton balls to create sheep.

5 Finish the picture by making some paper flowers and a shining Sun. Stick them into place using your glue.

The Life of a Seed

It may seem like new plants shoot up overnight, but they take some time to grow fully. Make this fun seed guide to remind yourself of all the steps a seed takes to turn into a blossoming flower.

You will need:
- A piece of paper
- 4 large seeds or beans
- Glue
- colored card stock
- Scissors

1

Fold a piece of paper in half, and in half again, lengthways. This will make four equal-sized rectangular boxes. Open out the paper.

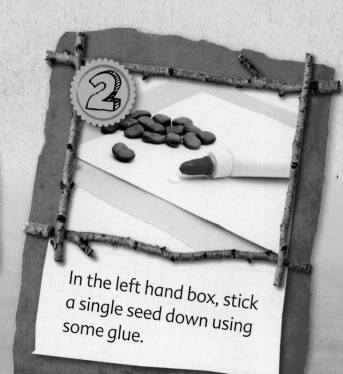

2

In the left hand box, stick a single seed down using some glue.

3

In the next box along, stick down another seed. Draw a small shoot onto green card stock and cut it out. Stick it above the seed.

4

Stick a seed in the next box along. Draw a larger shoot onto green card stock and cut it out. Draw a small bud on lighter green card stock. Stick both the shoot and the bud above the seed.

5

In the last box, stick down the final seed. Make a really long shoot out of green card stock. Draw petals on another card stock and stick everything above the seed to create a flower.

Leaf Print Flowers

Lots of sunlight and spring showers are the perfect combination to help plants grow. You may even find that they grow so big that they need to be trimmed back. Next time you are in the garden or a park, collect pruned leaves to do some printing.

You will need:

- Leaves
- Acrylic paint
- Paper plate or paint pallet
- A piece of paper
- Paintbrush

Select some leaves that are different shapes; some short and round and some long and thin.

Apply paint onto a flat surface, such as a paper plate. Use a paintbrush to spread the paint out in a thin layer.

3

Press a short, round leaf gently into the paint and print it onto a piece of paper. Leave lots of space around each print.

4

Using a long, thin leaf, press it gently into a different color paint. Print six leaf shapes around one of the short round shapes.

5

Repeat this for each of the short, round shapes. You can use different colors for each flower to make your artwork as colorful as possible.

Daffodil Paperweight

One of the earliest flowers to bloom in spring is the daffodil. Bring this pretty flower into your home by making a daffodil paperweight!

You will need:

- Egg carton segment
- Pebble
- Glue
- Yellow felt
- Orange marker
- Scissors
- Scrap paper
- Pen

Use an orange marker to color in the egg carton segment. Set aside.

Do you know any other flowers that blossom early in spring?

Draw a petal shape onto a piece of paper. Cut this out to make a template.

3 Use the template to cut five yellow petals out of some felt.

4 Stick the five petals onto the pebble using glue.

5 Glue the egg carton segment into the center of the petals.

13

Bark Rubbing

Forests and woods are full of exciting things, but you should leave most of them where you found them. One way to take a piece of the forest home with you is by making bark rubbings of some of the trees you pass.

You will need:

- Paper
- crayons
- Thin card stock
- Glue stick
- Scissors
- Pen

1

Hold a piece of paper onto a tree trunk, and, using the side of a dark green crayon, rub it gently over the paper to reveal a rubbing of the tree beneath.

2

Repeat this three more times, using different colors: blue, brown and light green.

3 Stick the blue rubbings onto thin card stock using a glue stick.

4 Cut a trunk shape out of the brown rubbings and a tree canopy out of the light green rubbings. Stick them onto the blue rubbings.

5 Finish your picture by drawing the outline of a strip of grass onto the dark green rubbings. Cut it out and stick it onto the bottom of the paper.

Bouncing Bunnies

If you are lucky, you may be able to see bunnies in spring. They are very shy, so you'll have to be quiet and patient to spot them. You can create your own bunnies, so that you can look at them whenever you like!

You will need:
- Different-sized leaves
- Colored card stock
- White paint
- Paper plate or paint pallet
- Scissors
- Glue
- Googly eyes

1 Choose some leaves. Make sure some are small and round, some are big and round, and some are long and thin.

2 Paint a thin layer of white paint onto a flat surface such as a paper plate. Gently press the big round leaf into the paint and print it on the card stock.

3

Repeat with a smaller, round leaf, making sure the prints overlap.

4

Using the long, thin leaves, print two ears. You can print the bunny's feet and tail with your finger.

5

Stick a pair of googly eyes onto the big, round leaf print. Cut out when dry.

Twig Hanging

When you look out of your window, you may be able to spot bright green leaves sprouting on lots of trees. Be inspired by the colors you can see to make a twig hanging that you can use to decorate your room.

You will need:

- Twigs that you have gathered
- Brightly colored yarn

1 Choose two twigs that are the same length.

2 Using some yarn, tie them together so that they form a cross.

3 Wind the yarn once around each twig, repeating until you have covered a third of the sticks.

4 Attach a new color of yarn and repeat winding the wool around each twig. Use as many different colors as you like.

5 When you reach the ends of the twigs, tie the yarn securely. Tie some yarn into a loop and attach it to the end of one twig.

Potted Flowers

These pretty spring flowers will stay in bloom all year! Ask an adult to help you find some flowers in your garden or the park. Place them in a piece of paper between two heavy objects to press them. Once they are dry, they are ready to use for this craft.

You will need:

- Press-dried flowers
- colored card stock
- Scissors
- Three green popsicle sticks
- Green craft foam
- Glue and glue stick
- Small stones or gravel
- clay pot

1 Choose three dried flowers that you want to use. Stick each of them onto different colored card stock.

2 Cut each of the flowers out and stick them on the end of a popsicle stick.

Cut out some leaf shapes and stem shapes from the craft foam. Stick them onto the popsicle sticks.

Fill a pot with some small stones.

Stick each of the popsicle stick flowers into the pot.

Soil Picture

Spring is the time when people sow seeds that grow into flowers, plants and even vegetables. They plant the seeds in the dark, rich soil. You can use some of this soil to make a fun bee picture!

You will need:

- Soil
- Yellow paper
- Pen
- Glue and paintbrush
- White paper
- Scissors
- Glue and glue stick
- Googly eyes

Using a pen, draw some oval shapes onto a yellow piece of paper. Draw stripes onto each of the oval shapes. Add a sting to each of the shapes.

In each oval, paint a thin layer of glue onto every other stripe.

3 Sprinkle some soil over the wet glue and shake off the excess.

4 Cut out some paper wings and stick them onto each bee.

5 Stick a googly eye onto each bee.

Always wash your hands after touching soil!

Glossary

bark (BARK) The rough outer layer of a tree's trunk and branches.

germinate (JER-muh-nayt) When a seed germinates, it begins to develop, growing a stem, leaves and roots.

hatch (HACH) When an animal breaks out of an egg.

prune (PROON) To trim a tree or bush.

sapling (SAP-ling) A young tree.

sow (SOH) To plant seeds in the ground.

template (TEM-plut) A shape you can draw around again and again to make the same shape.

Index

Further Reading

Appleby, Alex. *What Happens in Spring?* Four Super Seasons. New York: Gareth Stevens, 2014

Barnham, Kay. *Spring*. Seasons. New York: PowerKids Press, 2011.

Websites

For web resources related to the subject of this book, go to: www.windmillbooks.com/weblinks and select this book's title.